the book of rabbits

the book of rabbits

poems by
vince trimboli

~2019~

The Book of Rabbits
© Copyright 2019 Vince Trimboli
All rights reserved. No part of this book may be used or reproduced in any manner whatsoever without written permission from either the author or the publisher, except in the case of credited epigraphs or brief quotations embedded in articles or reviews.

Editor-in-chief
Eric Morago

Associate Editors
José Enrique Medina, Michael Miller

Marketing Specialist
Ellen Webre

Proofreader
Jim Hoggatt

Front cover art
"The Rabbit" by Michael Doig

Book design
Michael Wada

Moon Tide logo design
Abraham Gomez

The Book of Rabbits
is published by Moon Tide Press

Moon Tide Press #166
6745 Washington Ave.
Whittier, CA 90601
www.moontidepress.com

FIRST EDITION
Printed in the United States of America

ISBN #978-1-7339493-1-6

for Sara

Contents

Foreword by Nancy Lynée Woo 7

Hare 15
Wild: Young 16
First Dream 17
The Symptoms of a Breeding Woman 18
Haiku: Seeking (25yo, illiterate, female) 19
Why She Birthed Rabbits... 20
The Biology of Belief 21
What Miracles Have You Performed Today 22
Haiku: Facts about Birth 23
Field Guides: Interpretation 24
This Is a Story About Poverty 26
Her Forests in the City... 27
Men's Bodies Are Interesting.. 28
Haiku: Who Makes a Mother 29
Flopsy, Mopsy, and Cottontail 30
The Second Dream
   (Of the Possibility of Reality Television Stardom) 31
Haiku: Anatomy.. 32
The Impending Possibility of End Times 33
and What It Says About Rabbits... 33
Empathy is a Drink Best Served [ ]... 34
Her Doctors Caucus on the Damage Done to Her Body 35
Ink Blot 36
Haiku: Things Kept in Jars 37
The Third Dream (On the Possibility of Finding Treasure) 38
Jackal, Jackal... 39
Notes from a Field Trip to the Slaughterhouse 40
The Fourth Dream: Deus Ex Machina 41
Mythologies.. 42
A Hunger 43

About the Author 44
Notes and Acknowledgments 45

Foreword

In 1726, a poor, illiterate 25-year-old English peasant named Mary Toft captured the imagination of an entire country, making headlines with a claim to supernatural motherhood. Over the course of about two months, Toft gave birth to more than 15 dead rabbits, a liverless cat, a hog's bladder, and the body parts of other small creatures—or so she had all of England believing.

Toft executed these sensational births in front of the nodding heads of well-respected medical professionals. The top anatomist of the time, Nathaniel St. André, was so enthralled with the mystifying births that he published a 20-page paper entitled "A Short Narrative of an Extraordinary Delivery of Rabbets [sic]." She was brought to London as a captivating oddity. The King of England himself sent a doctor to investigate. But it wasn't until a porter was caught smuggling rabbit corpses into her room that she finally admitted she was in fact *manually inserting* the dead animals into her cervix and faking her labor pains.

Such is the uncanny premise for *The Book of Rabbits*, in which Vince Trimboli inhabits this bizarre narrative with an agile talent. A scientific theory of the time called maternal impression posited that Toft might have plausibly given birth to rabbits because she was emotionally obsessed with them while pregnant. The opening poem shows us the moment when Toft, having recently miscarried her fourth child, spots a rabbit in a field and starts "chasing the poor beast / until their bellies cramped." An eerie, unsettling quality runs throughout these poems, a delightfully perplexing itch under the skin, as Trimboli reimagines the story of Mary Toft and her fantastic births, often from her perspective, as if the story were true.

The poems focus keenly on Toft's inner world (which, for most women of the time, would rarely be heeded) as she experiences this disconcerting business of delivering rabbits. This is more than a book about an elaborate hoax, though it is certainly that. It is also a book about women, poverty, and the capacity of the human mind to believe the impossible. These poems, beautifully dreamlike and surreal, are more than slightly troublesome. They are as disquieting as the thought of a young woman actually stuffing dead rabbits into her body.

What could drive someone to do such a thing? Each poem takes a different stab at some kind of an answer. Was it grief for her unborn child, "weeping.../ for its stillness" that inspired Toft to fill that void with other creatures, roughly the size of a newborn, "her body becoming useful" once again? Was the crushing weight of poverty and "hunger for meats too rich for her purse" reason enough to stage such a scene? Was it a bold madness, a determined desire to "be more than a field-girl" and enter the slightly higher social ranks of freakshow curiosity? Was it a desire to be seen?

Perhaps "this was her idea of revenge for not being invited to her junior prom." The layer of genius I most enjoy about *The Book of Rabbits* is the seamless, disarming, creepy-crawliness of superimposing Toft's story upon a modern backdrop. Suddenly, in some instances, Toft is a woman "of a certain class" shopping "in the aisles of Kroger," or a waitress "double checking her pockets" as the "sun rises / over the ketchup bottles in the windows." Wherever we are in time, the shadow of a rabbit flickers in every corner—tuft of fur here, faint breathing there, subtle reminders of the haunting nature of desperation. The images nag at your sense of order, a unique display of magical realism. The lines between fantasy and reality are blurry, vein of melancholy running alongside an artery of hope.

The Book of Rabbits is a scrumptiously written response to a 300-year-old tabloid, provoking an exploration of the human capacity for wonder. Maybe Toft's ploy is not so different than any of the headlines we read in the checkout line of the grocery store. Or any stranger than a mentally ill woman "crad[ling] a jug of antifreeze," calling it a baby. Perhaps what she did is not any more foolish than a teenager ingesting laundry detergent for views on his YouTube channel. How powerful the mind is, how immense our willing gullibility, how strong our need for social recognition.

This book is a treat. I encourage you to savor the impressions, embrace the strangeness, and lean into the discomfort. I wouldn't be surprised if you ended up doing your own research on Mary Toft and her incredible delivery of rabbits, and then returned to this book with a deeper sense of appreciation. In fact, I recommend it. The details in this collection are rich and savory, morsels of fancy worth an informed reading.

Even so, I hope this introduction will have given you at least enough background to take pleasure in Trimboli's exquisite visions of Toft and his warmhearted renderings of this puzzling circumstance, naturally culling to the surface questions about the meaning of desire. Sure enough, through Trimboli's eyes, Toft is a sympathetic character. We see not only the grotesque and laughable ruse, but the power of one woman's daring plea, and the small, strange mark she left on history. The accomplishment here is nothing short of dramatic, turning expectations inside out, page after page. Enjoy.

— Nancy Lynée Woo
Long Beach, 2019

*The last bonfire that I come to
Myself I will cast in.*

— Lady Maisry, Traditional

*And the rabbit, because he cheweth the cud, but divideth
not the hoof; he is unclean unto you.*

— Leviticus, 11:6

From Guildford comes a strange, but well attested piece of News. That a poor Woman who lives at Godalmin, near that Town, who has a husband and two Children now living with her; was, about a Month past, delivered by Mr. John Howard, an eminent Surgeon and Man-Midwife living at Guildford, of a Creature resembling a Rabbit.

*— Weekly Journal or British Gazeteer,
Monday 10 October 1726*

Hare

The woman hath made an oath, that two months ago, being working in a field with other women, they put up a rabbit

— from the explanation given by Mary Toft

Dutiful in her labor

Five weeks gone and craving
meats too rich for her purse

The field as gold as ever

She reached down to her stomach
                then lower still

The swell above bone

      then spotted
      a hare

The child growing inside
willed her legs to churn beneath her skirt

Flint gray streak of lightning
across the noon sun

They chased her for no reason

Not to eat
Not to drape
her fur across her shoulders

Chasing the poor beast
until their bellies cramped
from running

their lips dried
from April's air

Wild: Young

Dear father. My footing is yet to be stable. My fur is nearly thick enough to cover the inside of my thighs or the scoop between my arm and breast. I am still fair there, still dewy. My feet still webbed, slightly. Am I still to be yours? A daughter or another beast of some new owner. Will the firebird hood give way to my back? When the sun shines down on my naked breast will modesty creep around my neck like a choker of gold? Give me this moment to catch my breath, let my knees buckle in. Let my arms push me up and be long. Give me one more trip around the sun to be wild, to be seventeen. Give me what is mine first. Let me find it. Let me reach in here, here, here.

First Dream

Fairly certain that this was a prophecy.

Of witchcraft, there are two dueling schools.

Science, that says a body is for producing.

Devotion, which is to say roses are for smelling.

Existential theory observed under bleachers.

Had Joshua lost interest in her?

What of the white rabbit?

She watched the way he looked at Virginia.

The expectation of finding her gutted.

That God has stopped watching.

With careful finger, she found the thing's spine,

found the tip of her own, too.

Had she been weeping

with hunger,

or for its stillness?

The Symptoms of a Breeding Woman

For women of a certain class
show no signs of it

In the aisles of Kroger, sifting through
her cart figuring out what to put back

She cannot afford it

Swollen and arched
the children hang from her

like kudzu vines,
like mustard greens

invasive and suffocating

The deli meats shimmer in
their cases

like fire opals

The package of stolen bologna
tucked between her legs

feels cold like a fish
her thighs unhooking it

In her purse: three dollars,
a half-snubbed butt of the cheapest cigarette

a number for a hotline
and not enough change

to call it

Haiku: Seeking (25yo, illiterate, female)

To bear this burden
Although you cannot read this
Must be good with kids

Why She Birthed Rabbits

Perhaps this was her idea of revenge for not being invited to her junior prom. Suitors her age longed for girls who had never woken up, pooled and ready to push. Her night shirts had long been stained with milk, and boys wanted crisp white V-necks, sleeves to roll their pack of cigarettes in, the other exposing their underarm as they reached up, punching the invisible face of their fathers. Perhaps she had been tired of being unnoticed by them. Pitched on picnic benches, knees hugged up to her chin. Was this to escape a life? She had wanted to dance to a slow song. What she wanted was her body to be hers again. Then, maybe she would be hers again. Birthing rabbits is a strange ordeal. No one ever gives you corsages after.

The Biology of Belief

The cubs are born thirty days later, in a litter of no more than five. Newborn cubs are a shapeless lump of white flesh, with no eyes or hair, though the claws are visible. The mother bear gradually licks her cubs into their proper shape, and keeps them warm by hugging them to her breast and lying on them, just as birds do with their eggs.

— *Pliny The Elder: Natural History book 8, 54*

Perhaps she watched
Who Framed Roger Rabbit.

Found a Little Golden Book
in the free bin

A placebo of her own making
cooked up in the field behind the Esso station

where she watched them,
warren of playful creatures

Watched the fox slink in
and tear them apart

What was left
matted with blood and dew

Tiny tufts of hide scattered:
Abandoned buggy, some bones

What Miracles Have You Performed Today

Jenny French kissed Albert under the overpass

Martha came home with two hickeys

Jane healed her bruised eye with prayer

Her father managed to escape jail time

Mary washed Jesus' feet with her hair

Louisa didn't have to fake it for once

Simone felt beautiful for the first time

News travels fast

Bridgette wasn't the most [ ] for once

The bone of an eel

They looked at her finally

Her body becoming useful

Haiku: Facts about Birth

For six weeks after
The cervix will stay open
Postpartum change purse

Field Guides: Interpretation

Field Guide to Dream Interpretation

The motivation of all dream content is wish-fulfillment, and that the instigation of a dream is often to be found in the events of the day preceding the dream, called "day residue."

— Freud

The simplest argument; that she had watched a rabbit and became overcome by her need to hold it. It's soft fur, almond eyes. They warn children that if you find a wild rabbit, to never touch it. The mother might abandon it once the scent of a human is on it. That petting something so small, for too long, might kill it. Evidence that loving something too much is both dangerous and deadly.

Field Guide to Animals Living at The Edge of the Meadow

Straying outland, creatures of great beauty inhabit Surrey's vast wilderness and woodlands. Species such as the rare Dartford warbler, nightjar, woodlark and tree pipit can be found to nest in both wooded areas and ground-lands. The varying habitats host a diverse mixture of wildlife, including roe deer, badgers and foxes.

This would be quite a different story had it been a deer that she spotted as she sat pecking at her modest lunch.

Field Guide for the Care and Well Being of Rabbits

Rabbits, not unlike most household pets, go through multiple shedding cycles a year. It's important that you brush your rabbit and remove all the excess fur during shedding cycles. Un-brushed rabbits can ingest excess fur, causing serious digestive issues.

Skinning any animal is an intimate act. Even the membrane that holds the thing together was once a living and breathing being. Placated. A more loving act than the gutting. Some say this is the easiest part of being human.

Field Guide to Birthing

Fluid gushing or leaking from the vagina means the membranes of the amniotic sac that surrounded and protected your baby have ruptured. This can occur hours before labor starts or during labor. Most women go into labor within 24 hours. If labor does not occur naturally during this time frame, doctors may induce labor to prevent infections and delivery complications.

— *WebMd*

What they don't tell you is that birthing doesn't end when the copay has been reached. The way they listen to you fight with their father, the glimpse of your naked and stretched body in the shower; These too are steps in the birthing process. Force them to take sides. When they visit Daddy, does he let them eat ice-cream for breakfast? Do they get to sleep through church? Whose side did you think they would take? Shelia looks better in her bathing suit on family vacations.

Field Guide to Sanity

* No entries have yet to be made on the subject.

Fortuitous happenings: For example, two holly trees, each of the opposite sex, grow within meters of one and other. The production of berries becomes eminent.

This Is a Story About Poverty

For the women who can afford them,
silicone babies can be purchased
from boutique websites.

Outside the Jewish Deli
a woman cradles an empty
jug of antifreeze;
Calls it "baby Chastity."

What's so strange about rabbits...

Her Forests in the City

On her first trip outside of Surrey, Mary packed light. In her carry-on, one change of clothes for the rare chance that she might stand in the presence of the king, a small jar (the contents, a lucky rabbit's foot), and a few dollars in case the city butcher didn't accept checks. Her eyes focused in on a *Redbook* to pass the time. Perhaps here, she thought, I might be more than a field-girl. Or at least, she thought, I might be asked if I need a moment to rest.

Men's Bodies Are Interesting

On mission trips to some South American countries, women
are instructed that they should bring plenty of tampons.

This is a very Catholic country,
the tour guide says.

When men put their bodies on the line
it is called bravery.

For women, the same act—
lunacy.

Good girls don't put things inside of them.

No one asks the flooding river why
people drown there.

Perhaps this is the biggest secret,
that any body can become dangerous;

With enough tow
even a stream can carry you away.

Haiku: Who Makes a Mother

That He was put there
No questions of Mary's tale
Crammed in while alone

Flopsy, Mopsy, and Cottontail
for Joshua, Mary Jr, Anne, and James's

For without convincing,
Peter (not a thief by nature)

might have been able to escape
the sentence of deviant.

Noted: He was hungry, poor,
without maternal love

And yes, this factors into
his apparent arrested development.

But what of poor Mr. McGregor?
What of his family in winter,

the ball jars empty.
His wife on a disability check

from the years
of maternal indignation.

*One more harvest like this
and I am moving in with my sister.*

He thinks of the rifle he keeps in the barn,
the record player.

Which of his children,
their dirt-streaked faces,
might find him first.

The Second Dream
(Of the Possibility of Reality Television Stardom)

Another night on this island
You planned your escape, applying

to another life until you aged-out
They never did want you

Girl, tanned by the light of the Esso station
Broad shoulders, never an intentional beauty

The smell of eggs on the stove
Too many lovers: Envy, hinges, knots of grass in your fists

Gray streak of lightning across the field,
centrifugal manifestation of longing

Your body, Mr. Nielsen,
to do with as you please

Of corporate sponsors: Products for women.
Make them noticeable again.

Give their husbands something
soft and keep-able.

Haiku: Anatomy

Magic tricks aside
This is not so far-fetched
Ask the clitoris

The Impending Possibility of End Times and What It Says About Rabbits

Chasms will open up in many places, and fire will be shot forth frequently. Wild beasts will roam beyond their territory, and women will give birth to monsters.t

— 2 Esdras 5:8

On Tuesday, the paternity tests come in manila envelopes. The audience revs itself up to a fever pitch at the encouragement of host A or maybe B depending on the channel. Does a swab of the cheek determine who chooses the wrench to remove the training wheels? Dutiful prophecy; He has his father's ears. Tuesdays are eventful days.

Empathy is a Drink Best Served [ ]
for S.

I am incredibly sad

I imagine she was too,
without

the ability to find comfort

not a trick of light

not the Midwest, its flatness

the promise of a storm
that never came

Her Doctors Caucus on the Damage Done to Her Body
a found poem in the voices of men who claim the best intentions for women's bodies

Q. What do you tell a woman with two black eyes?
A. Nothing that you haven't already told her!

Q: What's the most common sleeping position of a woman?
A: Around.

Q: What do you call a woman with no clitoris?
A: It doesn't matter, she's not going to come.

Q: How did the medical community come up with the term "PMS"?
A: "Mad Cow Disease" was already taken.

Q: What do women and a bar have in common?
A: Liquor in the front, poker in the back.

Q: How do you blind a woman?
A: You put a windshield in front of her.

Q: Why do women have periods?
A: Because they deserve them.

Ink Blot

The sheer silliness of it

To ask her what
she saw in it

If it could be anything else

Heavy-pooled around the crease
Two arms stretching up and out

A daughter reaching into dress sleeves

Her mother pushing the hair back
from exhaustion

No, not a Sunday scene like that...

more daughter than dress
                        More leg

Spindles, suspended mid-air

Perfectly mirrored, the both of them
Sides of stock, respectively

Haiku: Things Kept in Jars

She touched all of them
Each one a reminder that
all pearls are traumas

The Third Dream (On the Possibility of Finding Treasure)

Late night diner
Greek by the name on the menu

The booth filled to the brim:
Astrix, Sussex, Blanc de Bouscat

The exterminator at her feet peeks
between table and bench,

Tells her his plans of cashing in
his life savings to hunt treasure

*The next time you see me
will be on T.V. claiming my booty*

She believes him

Her coffee cup wishes him luck,
men have all of it anyways

As she finishes, the sun rises
over the ketchup bottles lined in the windows

Double checking her pockets,
time card, her own hand,

Packing her things, she thinks
of her treasures

In the field where she found them

Jackal, Jackal

There is very little to offer. She watches her daughter run through the single-wide, notices the bottoms of her feet stained with crud. In the single bedroom, the crashing of a lamp breaks her thinking, like a paper breaks a dog. Her hair breaking at the roots. There is still enough stillness left in her to put one hand over her eye, block out where she is standing, pretend for a split second [ ] She pulls herself off the couch, starting with her breath. Works her way up. The wingspan of a stork can reach nine and a half feet when fully mature. The average Jackal is only three feet in length. The setting sun sets, the storm-door left open. Take this as a gesture of hope. Take this as an offering for [ ]

Notes from a Field Trip to the Slaughterhouse

Industrious brevity. I too
walked into the room unwilling.

For the sake of [ ] we can
do unspeakable things.

Posing in the watch of the slaughterhouse
the children looked tiny.

The point of the trip was to teach them
about hunger.

They each wore three gossamer sacks.
One over their hair. One over each shoe.

Each wall still wet; fumes of union men
brought in to tidy things up a bit.

The point was never to scare them. Although,
fear is as much a part of hunger as the eating.

Each little face.

The room's center, haunted,
marked each ghost: Grate and drain.

I am looking for the center of something.
        I do not know where to skin it.

The Fourth Dream: Deus Ex Machina

What dress should she wear?

In other news, the King spoke
eerily into the camera about immigration.

She thinks, this will be good dinner conversation.

Hair still waiting to be set,
she lines her lips to keep them…

Dotty, who was hosting dinner, was known for being academically kooky.

High ball glasses, a cheese plate;
Something Richard shot and smoked.

With all the deductibles paid, she should have treated herself.

Settling in on something beige,
a brooch set with the birthstones of her children.

Tucked into her blouse, a locket stuffed with fur.

Dotty greeted them at the door,
forgotten rosewater lingering.

Can you believe that speech today?

None of us are really ever safe anymore.

The groomed lawn and sprinkler system:
Even the cul-de-sac looked delicious.

The wallpaper in the powder room, a fox hunt.

She pressed her ear to it
hoping to hear even faint breathing.

Mythologies

The fossils of trilobites can often be found in rock quarries and along riverbeds. Another lesson learned by the riding mower mangling a nest of wild rabbits in the side lot. She stoops down and dips her hands in the muck. There is time yet, to tell the little one about breathing, how it stops, about where babies [ ] In the marketplace, they try to peddle her fruits and soaps. There is no gold hidden anywhere. This is a lesson as well. For each hen, she has tugged and bled, she prayed first for signs of egg. Even after. For her littlest, a different mythology. For the dog, an easy meal that requires no chase.

A Hunger

The Charlatans. I am one of those. In January, the month the owls nest in. I am a witness & a small thing altogether.

— *Lucie Brock-Broido*

No more the porridge
        than the skin around her fingers

Wildness was just that
        a half moon under glass

How to be tethered, she thought
        Let the tulips die out this year

She asked the fire her name
        asked the newsman if he had children

If she could give herself another name:
        Luna-Buck, or Dear Helen

Could she ever eat Coq au Vin, Confit
        She called out, collect, to no answer

Last Spring, they gathered for dinner
        She will try again, then, when winter goes into hiding

About the Author

Vincent Trimboli is a Queer Appalachian Artist and Poet that holds a MFA in Creative Writing from West Virginia Wesleyan College. In 2016, Trimboli published two chapbooks with Ghost City Press (*Condominium Morte* and *other milkweed diners*). His poems can be found in *Connotation Press, Still Journal, The San Diego Reader, Cultural Weekly* as well as multiple print and online anthologies. Vince has taught Writing, Literature, and Public Speaking in a Medium/Maximum Security Prison in the hills of West Virginia and has been Adjunct Professor of English at many Colleges and Universities throughout his home state. Currently Vince lives in Elkins, WV.

Notes and Acknowledgments

In "What Miracles Have You Performed Today": The line, "The Bone from an eel," comes from medical records recording other objects birthed by Mary Toft.

The poem "Field Guides: Interpretation" is inspired by the form of "Notes on Ice in *Bowditch*" by Elizabeth Bradfield from her collection "Approaching Ice" (Persa Books, Inc., 2010).

The title "Men's Bodies Are Interesting" is borrowed from the poem "Let's Be Serious Now" by Mary Ann Samyn from the book "My Life In Heaven" (Oberlin College Press, 2013)

The poem "Flopsy, Mopsy, and Cottontail" is dedicated to the children and husband of Mary Toft.

The title and epigraph of the final poem comes from the book "A Hunger" by Lucie Brock-Broido (Knopf, 1988).

Patrons

Moon Tide Press would like to thank the following people for their support in helping publish the finest poetry from the Southern California region. To sign up as a patron, visit www.moontidepress.com or send an email to publisher@moontidepress.com.

Anonymous
Robin Axworthy
Conner Brenner
Bill Cushing
Susan Davis
Peggy Dobreer
Dennis Gowans
Half Off Books & Brad T. Cox
Jim & Vicky Hoggatt
Ron Koertge & Bianca Richards
Ray & Christi Lacoste
Zachary & Tammy Locklin
Lincoln McElwee
David McIntire
José Enrique Medina
Andrew November
Michael Miller & Rachanee Srisavasdi
Terri Niccum
Ronny & Richard Morago
Jennifer Smith
Andrew Turner
Mariano Zaro

Also Available from Moon Tide Press

Everything I Write is a Love Song to the World, David McIntire *(2019)*
Letters to the Leader, HanaLena Fennel (2019)
Darwin's Garden, Lee Rossi (2019)
Dark Ink: A Poetry Anthology Inspired by Horror (2018)
Drop and Dazzle, Peggy Dobreer (2018)
Junkie Wife, Alexis Rhone Fancher (2018)
The Moon, My Lover, My Mother, & the Dog, Daniel McGinn (2018)
Lullaby of Teeth: An Anthology of Southern California Poetry (2017)
Angels in Seven, Michael Miller (2016)
A Likely Story, Robbi Nester (2014)
Embers on the Stairs, Ruth Bavetta (2014)
The Green of Sunset, John Brantingham (2013)
The Savagery of Bone, Timothy Matthew Perez (2013)
The Silence of Doorways, Sharon Venezio (2013)
Cosmos: An Anthology of Southern California Poetry (2012)
Straws and Shadows, Irena Praitis (2012)
In the Lake of Your Bones, Peggy Dobreer (2012)
I Was Building Up to Something, Susan Davis (2011)
Hopeless Cases, Michael Kramer (2011)
One World, Gail Newman (2011)
What We Ache For, Eric Morago (2010)
Now and Then, Lee Mallory (2009)
Pop Art: An Anthology of Southern California Poetry (2009)
In the Heaven of Never Before, Carine Topal (2008)
A Wild Region, Kate Buckley (2008)
Carving in Bone: An Anthology of Orange County Poetry (2007)
Kindness from a Dark God, Ben Trigg (2007)
A Thin Strand of Lights, Ricki Mandeville (2006)
Sleepyhead Assassins, Mindy Nettifee (2006)
Tide Pools: An Anthology of Orange County Poetry (2006)
Lost American Nights: Lyrics & Poems, Michael Ubaldini (2006)